What's for Dinner?

Written by Sarah Prince
Illustrated by Liz Cogley

The lion asked the tiger.

The tiger asked the bat.

The bat asked the eagle.

The eagle asked the cat.

The cat asked the crocodile.

The crocodile asked the wolf.

The wolf asked the rabbit.

"What's for dinner?"